The Worst
FASHION
TRENDS
in the
World!

Richard Jarman
and the Advertising Archives

Contents

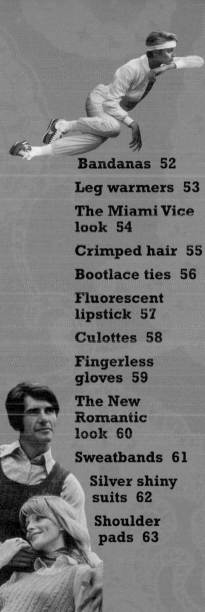

Introduction

Fashion, the current and popular style in dress, is by definition constantly changing. Fashion is always the 'new black'. And, like all things that alter, fashion can change either for the better or for the worse. This book isn't about the better. It's not about what's hot or even about what's not. Rather, it's about what should never have been in the first place, never mind last week, last month or last year!

You may ask who am I to sit in judgement on fashion? Well, you're not alone. I asked myself the same question. Hand on heart, I can't say I've any standing in the world of fashion. I possess no certificates in fabric-cutting, no tracing-paper designs, and I'm no wizard on the sewing machine either. Nor am I a dedicated follower of fashion: snoods and sweatbands may have gone round other people's heads, but as fashion trends I must confess they went completely over mine.

However, in my defence I can point to an early (and short-lived) career as a fashion model. It was in Birmingham in 1974 in the hall of a Methodist Mission. My brother Phil and I were sent down

4

a catwalk dressed in nothing but matching nylon vests and underpants by my mother, who was then an agent for a now-defunct mail-order line called Pandora, the clothing equivalent of Tupperware. Terrified and humiliated, we held hands as we padded furtively down the catwalk through rows of grinning onlookers. It's an experience I've never forgotten, and although I swore from then on that I'd had my fill of the fashion world, I must admit to harbouring a voyeuristic pleasure in the fashion humiliations of others.

Given that this book looks back into recent history, the fact that I'm qualified as a historian of sorts, with a degree under my belt to prove it, is another useful string to my bow. No doubt in these days of 24/7 news and rent-a-quote chat-show comments, I could be considered a 'fashion expert' (or 'fashionologist') given that I've already written this book by the time you're reading it, and therefore qualified to lord my opinions on daytime TV or the Shopping Channel.

In any case, this book's about ordinary fashion, and not only am I very ordinary, I can also lay claim to having experienced the worst fashion excesses of each of the decades covered in this book. For example, I wore flares and a parka snorkel in the '70s; I had a curly perm and a batwing stonewashed denim jacket in the '80s; and I even looked like something that had crept out of a rubbish skip in the grungy '90s. Like most of the '60s generation, I too remember little about that decade, but that's because I was a baby, while others have only marijuana and LSD to blame. Having said that, I'm sure that my mum, armed with her Pandora baby collection, saw to it that I wasn't lacking in bad fashion in that decade either.

While we're on the subject of the '60s, let me explain why this book starts there. This is not a definitive history of fashion no-nos, encompassing everything from the Roman toga, the Elizabethan codpiece and the Edwardian whalebone corset. There is a school of thought that argues that fashion trends, as we understand them today, only really came about in the post-war period, and in the '60s in particular. While I accept that there are deficiencies in this argument, I did want to cover the subject within 90 pages, making that particular school of thought very attractive and one to which I'm nailing my colours firmly, albeit more out of necessity than conviction.

You may think that these fashions have more of the random jumble sale about them than a carefully compiled collection. While I can't say that I selected these on objective criteria, I wasn't wholly subjective either. I've adopted the 'Elephant' test approach: I know a fashion corker when I see one. I admit that this is not a particularly strict test, but it is a test nevertheless. In the true sense of the philistine, I might not know much about fashion, but I know what I like.

Here's one cheap way to make
the Minilands Chatsworth, £74 and up.

This is the Yeti at £88
The whole thing is quite monstrous.

I set myself ground rules, too. For example, I decided to stick to inanimate objects only, namely clothing in all its forms, accessories and hairstyles, with a bit of make-up thrown in. Anything with a pulse, such as adopted Romanian babies, little yappy dogs or Japanese girlfriends were ruled strictly out of bounds, although I do accept that all of the aforementioned have at one time or another been fashion 'must-haves'. I also ruled out fashion trends in behaviour or social conduct, such as snorting cocaine or joining suicidal cults. I wanted something altogether more tangible at which I could shake my stick.

Secondly, the fashion had to be a 'trend' as opposed to a fad, a tendency more than a mere gimmick. I was looking for patterns rather than puffs and fancies, though I fancy you'll see a few puffs as you flick through these pages. To this end, I have concentrated on more long-term movements in the fashion market. For example, I threw out one-offs such as Michael Jackson's single silver-sequinned glove and Geri Halliwell's Union Jack dress as not being trends in the real sense of the word.

I've also insisted on some semblance of mass appeal. While sneering at the Goth uniform, the accoutrements of which are nowadays purchasable in Claire's Accessories and Miss Selfridge, it cannot be described as a mass trend. The same goes for the worse

fashion excesses of glam rock; although having made more of a connection with the mainstream than the Goths did, glam rock was actually self-deprecating, flaunted by those who were in on the joke. To include it here would be to admit a sense-of-humour failure.

Looking at the worst fashion trends that cleared the hurdles mentioned above, it was interesting to see how certain themes kept cropping up:

• Pretentiousness figured highly. In this category, I include bandanas, baseball caps worn backwards and ironically worn dungarees; they were over-egging the point and trying too hard.

• A sense of being out of place appeared again and again. In here, I've lumped Afghan coats and the '80s Miami Vice look, which were more suited to the climates of Afghanistan and Miami respectively than, say, a rainy day in Kidderminster. I also extended this to embrace ski pants, more suited to snow than show.

• 'Ill-fitting' and 'impractical' are descriptions that occurred over and over. In this category, I've included angel sleeves, puffa jackets, kaftans, pinafores, baggy jeans, culottes, smocks and the dreaded tube socks.

• Another related grouping is the plain ugly, styles that made us look aesthetically gross and unattractive by any objective yardstick. In this section, I've condemned basin haircuts,

batwing sweaters, lamb-chop sideburns, bum bags, goatees, moon boots and stonewashed jeans.

• There's also a category I refer to as the 'Jurassic Park bad science idea': just because we have the science and the wherewithal to create a fashion doesn't mean that we should actually make it – and then wear it! For examples, see mood rings, colour-change T-shirts and plastic dresses.

• Female-to-male fashion doesn't travel well, I found, as the wardrobe of any common-or-garden transvestite or jobbing drag-queen will testify. Here I've included sarongs for men, clogs and shaggy perms. Funnily enough, the vice versa, male to female, doesn't figure at all (if we don't count the masculine shoulder pads of the '80s, that is).

• Clothes that age us don't win any fashion bonus points: peasant dresses, granny gowns and fur-lined pixie boots had the unfortunate effect of making 12-year-olds look more like their great-great aunts, now deceased.

• The reverse is also true. If it's flogged to teenyboppers, then it's flogged to death in fashion terms. Producing it in child sizes is the death knell to a fashion trend – see fingerless gloves, ra-ra skirts and leg warmers.

• When the wrong people start to consume a particular trend en masse, it's in trouble, particularly when it's the fatties squeezing into the tiniest of costumes. Here we remember boob tubes, leggings and cycling shorts, lest we forget.

• Garishness is a bad omen too, so in went Bermuda shorts, Hawaiian shirts and polka dots.

• 'Downright silly' doesn't feature highly on the fashion Richter scale, and into this bin I've thrown non-matching neon socks, appliqué on jumpers, parachute pants, cravats and the eternally pointless pom-pom.

• Hairdos requiring high maintenance aren't conducive to good fashion either. The fashion equivalents of road-kill that have sprung from DIY hairstyling should serve as fitting epitaphs to the home perm kit and the crimping tongs.

• Finally, I have a miscellaneous catch-all category into which I've swept the lowest of the low. Wallowing at the bottom of the fashion equivalent of Dante's Inferno, I have made a judge's special Worst Fashion Award to the shell suit, the mullet and the poncho.

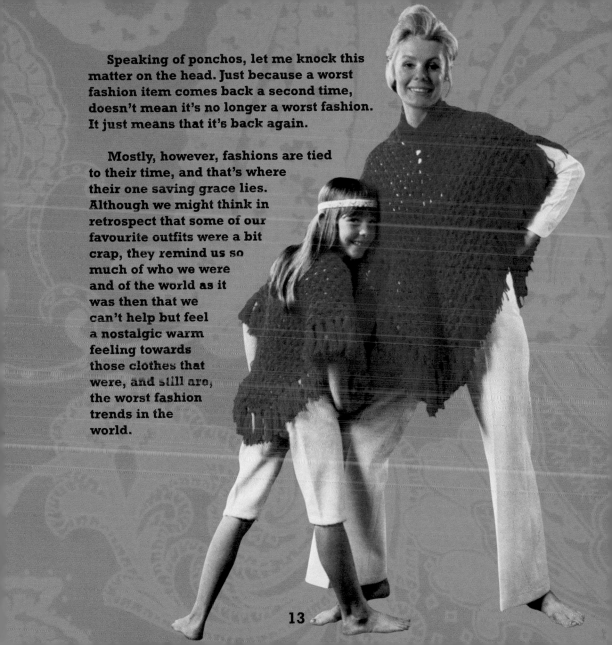

Speaking of ponchos, let me knock this matter on the head. Just because a worst fashion item comes back a second time, doesn't mean it's no longer a worst fashion. It just means that it's back again.

Mostly, however, fashions are tied to their time, and that's where their one saving grace lies. Although we might think in retrospect that some of our favourite outfits were a bit crap, they remind us so much of who we were and of the world as it was then that we can't help but feel a nostalgic warm feeling towards those clothes that were, and still are, the worst fashion trends in the world.

13

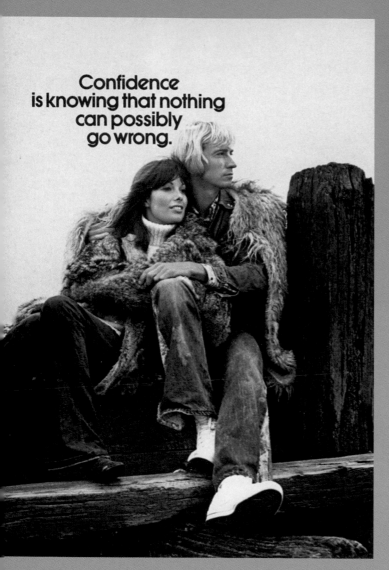

Confidence
is knowing that nothing
can possibly
go wrong.

AFGHAN COATS

Afghan coats were the anti-war movement's uniform in its fight against the carpet-bombing of Vietnam. Unfortunately, they also made the protestors look like carpets — or Big Bird. If it rained, these furry fashion warriors became heavy, wet and matted, and resembled sheep emerging from an anti-parasite dip. More suited to a freezing night inside the caves of Tora Bora than a shopping precinct, here the guy's Afghan has met its match in his hairdo.

PAISLEY

Pretty big in the '60s, with a comeback of sorts in the early '90s, paisley was always awful. The teardrop-like splodges that are the hallmark of paisley are what alien sperm must look like under the microscope, or leeches on LSD. That Paisley is also the name of the most depressing town in Scotland could not benefit its fashion namesake, nor indeed does its association with the artist sometimes known as Prince.

PATCHWORK

In 1969, patchwork was liberated from old ladies' bedspreads and was strutting proudly down the catwalk as vogue. It was like a hand grenade had gone off at a jumble sale and somehow every piece of cloth had been randomly stitched back together again. Jeans, shirts and skirts were coming out in mixtures of denim, cotton, velvet and corduroy, and needlework groups everywhere were seizing control. But we still looked like old ladies' blankets on the loose.

ALICE BANDS

There's something too 'Little Miss Goody Two-Shoes' about Alice bands, the essential accessory of the '80s Lady Diana (or Sloane Ranger) look. You got the feeling that the sickly sweet exterior masked a deranged psychopath. This particular devil-child is the mutant offspring of Anne of Green Gables and a vampire and looks more Alice Cooper than Alice through the Looking Glass. Here, she has just spat green matter at a crucifix after an exorcism by a visiting priest.

17

PLASTIC DRESSES

Man-made materials were cutting-edge technology in the '60s, so it wasn't long before someone made a plastic dress. Easy to wipe down with a wet cloth should the need arise, the plastic dress's downsides outweighed its positives and hastened its demise; not only did you sweat buckets, but you had to keep clear of naked flames and electrical appliances. One spark and your plastic dress would go up like a torch. Talk about a burning bush…

TUBE SOCKS

As the sock without a foot, the tube sock had no heel and instead was just that: a tube. After one day's wear, it became vaguely foot-shaped, but not so that you could tell which way was the right way round. Ultimately, tube socks resulted in unsightly bags and bulges, so that you looked like an old lady with crumpled stockings. Better suited to outdoor walking expeditions such as trekking through a peat bog than to the catwalk, tube socks went over the knee and tended to come striped with silly colours.

Get it on with Vincel and cotton... the big, big fabric happening on the young Spring fashion scene. In feel-free textures and come-on colours. Get it on. Feel cool. And you've got it made.

COURTAULDS Vincel

LAMB-CHOP SIDEBURNS

In the late '60s, men grew lion manes and their whiskers turned lamb chop. Guys everywhere started looking like Dickensian work-house overseers. Facial hair hadn't been so popular since the Neanderthal Age, only these cavemen were tottering about in Cuban heels and tight pants, a retrograde step in evolutionary terms, perhaps. Every wannabe hunk patiently grew his lamb chops with the sort of dedication he would use in later life for ornamental hedge-trimming.

GRANNY GOWNS

These were big in the '70s. Literally. Usually worn as party frocks by everyone from young girls to older women, granny gowns made you look like a marquee that had come loose from its guide pegs. Or a ship in full sail. Usually floral patterned with frilly hems and bits of random embroidery, they were more suited to burying old grannies in than to going out on the town.

BASIN HAIR

The only fashion style to come from the Middle Ages and about as aesthetically pleasing as the Black Death or the pox, 'the basin' was very simple to achieve: put basin on head, apply scissors around basin, take off basin, spray down. A helmet of a hairdo if ever there was one – or should we say hair-don't? And what an imaginative use for a doily...

BELL-BOTTOMS

By 1975, trousers had reached bell-bottom proportions. They were so wide at the bottom that you could stand a small person up in your trouser leg. Men wore bell-bottoms so tight that you could not only tell their religion, but also whether they were pleased to see you. The problem with bell-bottoms was that if you walked through a puddle on the way to work, the resulting capillary action would provide you with a wet crotch by lunchtime.

For whom the bells toll.

PATONS

to knit

2164 8

Tank Tops
33-40 in. (84-101 cm)

and crochet

TANK TOPS

The world went tank-top crazy in the '70s. These knitted sleeveless sweaters were often peeled down tightly over equally tight-fitting shirts, usually with long collars, as modelled by the His & Hers couple on the right. They're showing off tank tops that they made themselves from old bathroom mats — they now earn cash in hand as moving targets for their local amateur air-rifle club.

PONCHOS

The poncho is, by any other name, a piece of blanket with a hole in the middle. Wearing one is like putting your head through the top of a wigwam to go down to the shops. A difficult look to get right, when a poncho goes wrong, it really goes wrong. Some ponchos look like something found in a dog's basket, others, such as the hand-knitted ponchos modelled here, were usefully deployed as netting on Icelandic sea-trawlers during the Cod Wars.

POM-POMS

Like the fuzzy things cheerleaders wave about at American ball games, pom-poms seem somehow a bit too silly and cute. Over the years, pom-poms have found their way onto the tops of woolly hats, sweaters and even, God forbid, ponchos. There's something far too nursery about pom-poms. Look at these two cutey-pies: are they wearing pom-poms on their hats, or are they sporting the trophies of a recent polar-bear castration?

PINAFORES

A collarless, sleeveless dress worn over a shirt or sweater, the pinafore was the mother of home overalls, better suited to churning butter than high-street chic. The pinafores pictured come in Russian-doll sizes: each one coming out of the other in a dress size smaller than the last. The lady on the left is about to hatch a smaller pinafore while her larger friend smiles at seafaring vessels sailing by.

CLOGS

The traditional footwear of Dutch cheese-makers and the industrial poor, clogs enjoyed a revival in the late '70s, bizarrely, among men. A slip-on shoe with a thick wooden sole, man-clogs gave much-needed height to shorties and were very affordable. However, they still looked lumpy as we clattered through the neighbourhood in them. One kick to a football and both ball and clog would be projected through next-door's front window.

WET-LOOK MACS

Wet-look macs were made of crumpled patent leather or plastic. It could be drought weather in which even the cockroaches gave up the will to live, but wet-look macs still made us look as if we'd just stepped out of a rainstorm or had taken a tumble in the bath. And what was so wrong with a fashion that made us look wet, soggy, sodden, dripping, half-soaked, drenched, a drip and as sexy as a wet Wednesday? Well, there again…

CRAVATS

Cravats were androgynous, and maybe that's what was so wrong about them. They made us look like a bizarre hybrid of the macho lady-killer and something that was altogether too feminine and camp. This example is a paisley version of a cravat, the shape of which wouldn't have looked out of place in a Second World War bomber command or the Hitler Youth. See how it matches the rest of the shirt in that '70s way of matching patterns. Mmm. Nice.

THE 'FARRAH'

Farrah Fawcett fell to earth in the '70s as a Charlie's Angel. Her wings disintegrated on impact and women's hair the world over was instantly feathered. Creating a triangle at the forehead with lots of flip and lots of hairspray, the 'Farrah' flick demanded the destruction of the ozone layer and the melting of the polar caps. Some 'Farrahs' went off on perm/feathered combo tangents of their own to equally catastrophic effect, like this one we prepared earlier...

ANGEL SLEEVES

Not satisfied with trouser ends, bell-bottoms moved up to infect sleeves. More frou-frou and chintzy than practical, angel sleeves looked like those '70s lace curtains in bedroom windows, gathered up in festoons. Dinner party hostesses everywhere got their sleeves coated in prawn-cocktail sauce while dishing out the melon boats. Billowing out at the slightest suggestion of a breeze, angel sleeves had a windsock appearance – it's amazing no one accidentally navigated a 747 down to earth by swinging their arms around.

HOT PANTS

Hot pants should have only been worn by anorexics weighing two pounds above organ failure but, like all worst fashions, women of every shape and size took up the challenge of squeezing themselves in. If all the shoppers in the changing rooms at Dorothy Perkins had collectively breathed in to get into their hot pants, the windows would have imploded. How everyone sighed with relief when ankle-slimming maxi-skirts came back and they could eat chips again.

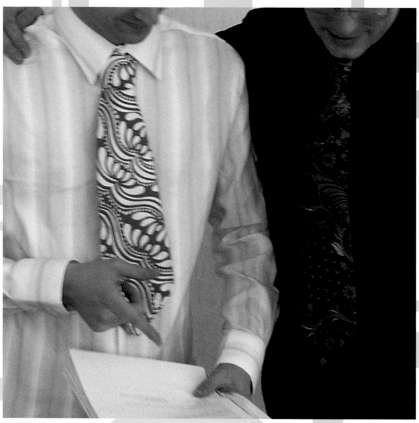

KIPPER TIES

So called because they looked like kippered herrings hanging in a fishmonger's window, in fashion terms, kipper ties stank even more. A cravat-like form of a tie, kippers were usually patterned in garish stripes and colours and always came in cheap-looking fabrics. The trend was either to clash the kipper with an equally gaudy shirt or, even worse, to match a kipper tie pattern exactly with the one on the shirt. Who needs LSD when you've colour coordinations like these?

MOUSTACHES

Hey Gringo! These were the moustaches of real men, the sort of
guys who hung out in bars, wore leather caps and jackets and had
their backside hanging out of a pair of chaps. How many dads must
have shaved off their moustaches after they saw The Village People
prancing about singing YMCA on TV? Nowadays, the facial hair
mostly favoured by military dictators, moustaches are incredibly
hilarious: look, she's pissing herself laughing.

PARKAS

Coming in navy blue, green and sometimes silver, snorkel parkas were worn by boys in the '70s. The lining was always bright space-hopper orange, and the fur round the hood was genuine trapped and skinned synthetic fibre. When zipped up fully, the hood made a sort of trunk-like tube, giving the wearer the appearance of an elephant or a submarine periscope. The resulting tunnel vision and loss of hearing led many a '70s boy under the tyres of an oncoming juggernaut.

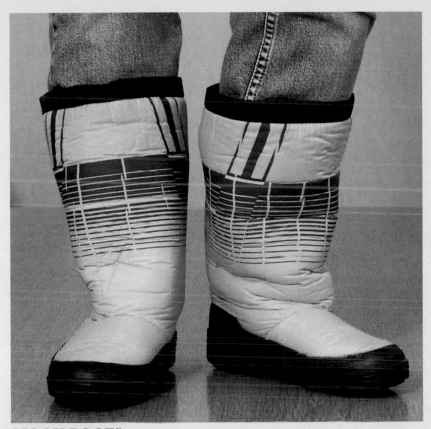

MOON BOOTS

These were heavy snow boots with elephantine treads and thick padding, usually gathered at the top with a cord, the sort of thing Neil Armstrong would have found useful, or Princess Leia in *Star Wars*. For some reason they became the urban footwear of choice in the early '80s. One bizarre offshoot of this phase was the shaggy and hairy style, like someone had hobbled Chewbacca or Big Foot himself. Uggs are the modern version; they're still horrible.

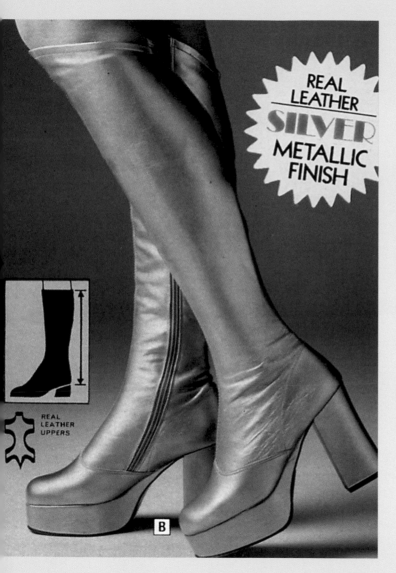

REAL
LEATHER
SILVER
METALLIC
FINISH

REAL
LEATHER
UPPERS

B

PLATFORMS

In the '70s, platform shoes became very fashionable, as did broken and twisted ankles. It was like having to walk about on built-in stilts and non-wearers felt like they'd shrunk a foot overnight. Platforms reached about four inches at the heel. Some people even got handymen to drill holes through the sole base to create shoes known as 'yo-yos'. But these shoes were never the easiest things to walk in and left us moving like we were wearing nappies. Not a sexy look.

SMOCKS

Doesn't this look like one of those apron- or tabard-things that your mum hung on the washing line to hold her clothes pegs? In the '70s, smocks were very big, in more senses than one. Ill-shaped and ill-fitting, if this was fashion hell then it had patterned flowers and big pockets too. The sort of thing you would want to wear only if you were a bus conductor or pregnant.

STARSKY CARDIGANS

Starsky and Hutch gave the world more than just screeching cars and platform shoes. Everyone loved them and wanted to get into their clothes. When David Soul sang 'Don't give up on us, baby', girls screamed to get into his pants. By way of contrast, Paul Michael Glaser was fighting off screaming men clawing to get into his chunky hand-knit cardigan with brown horizontal pattern and accompanying knitted belt. Wonder who got the bum deal?

ROCK HAIR

Rock hair is the original shit-for-hair, yet everyone who was anyone was hairy in the '70s. Here these lovely lads are holding their annual Leo Sayer look-alike reunion. Things didn't improve in the '80s, either. We thought our lacquered bouffant made us look just like Axl Rose or a stadium axe mutha from a group like Poison or Motley Crue; but we didn't, we looked just like that rock chick from Starship. Or Bonnie Tyler.

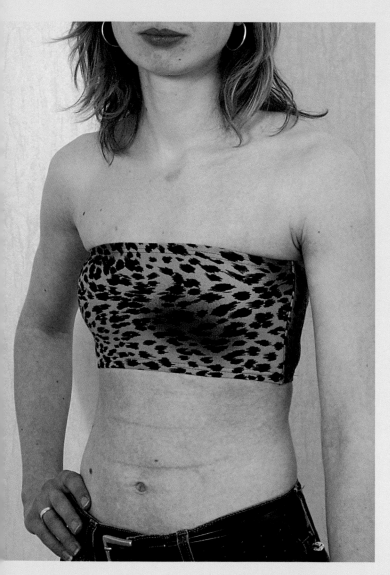

BOOB TUBES

Number one fashion tip: if it rhymes, don't wear it. Worn, usually by teenagers, without a bra, leaving the midriff, the top of the back and the shoulders bare. Favoured in the '70s disco era alongside tight spandex bell-bottoms, the most common variety came in spangled sequins.

Unfortunately, some women looked more like the disco ball spinning above their heads than Donna Summer in one of these. In this instance, we have stretch leopard. Lovely.

KAFTANS

In the '70s, Indian kaftans were both comfort wear and so shapeless that they were a popular home-sewing project for those who couldn't make anything else. But what proved airy also tended to prove unflattering. A kaftan made you look like the awning on the side of a trailer, or the sort of thing a Bedouin family would use to set up home in. Shapeless unisex gowns with wide necklines, it's hard to know how anyone differentiated between the sexes — at the end of the day, we all looked like walking tablecloths.

Turn white in the sun this summer.

POLYESTER LOUNGE SUITS

In the 1975 film *Shampoo*, Warren Beatty played a gigolo hairdresser, and his hairy chest launched a million lounge suits. The flashy gleam of synthetic fabric, the wide lapels, the top shirt-button undone to reveal a medallion…. At first considered elegant yet comfortable, lounge suits soon became really tacky and the sort of thing old men wore to the social club. Some lounge suits were very loud and garish, but most seemed to come in a safari khaki-cum-beige colour.

THE PEASANT LOOK

In the '80s, the peasant look harked back to a golden age of farmyard serfdom and traditional ethnic costume. Women everywhere looked like members of the Latvian national folk dancing team — or a pair of dining-room curtains. Knee-high skirts had a saucy swinging look, and men started fantasizing about sex in haylofts. Here, the lady on the left has a religious theme going on and sports a 'Wise man's gold headband and shepherd's smock' combo as her tribute to the Nativity.

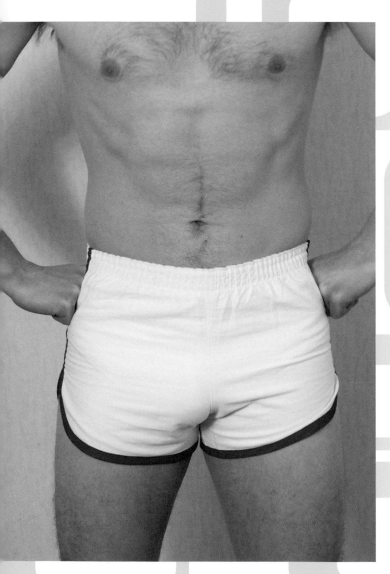

TRACK SHORTS

These sports shorts were really tight and had double stripes and tiny slits at the sides. More naked lunch than packed lunch, track shorts were minuscule. Every wannabe hunk hung about (and hung out) in a pair of these, and sperm counts in the western hemisphere plummeted. Eventually, the will to procreate became too much, as did the need for ventilation.

JUMPSUITS

Like a baby's romper suit in appearance, jumpsuits exploded in the '70s and '80s — a one-piece garment for the whole body of the kind usually worn by vermin-control or troops parachuting in on enemy territory. A plethora of useless zips, pockets and metal rings with one big zip up the middle, jumpsuits were less 'jump' and more 'lie around on the sofa eating Ferrero Rocher and watching *The Thorn Birds* and *Falcon Crest* on the VCR'.

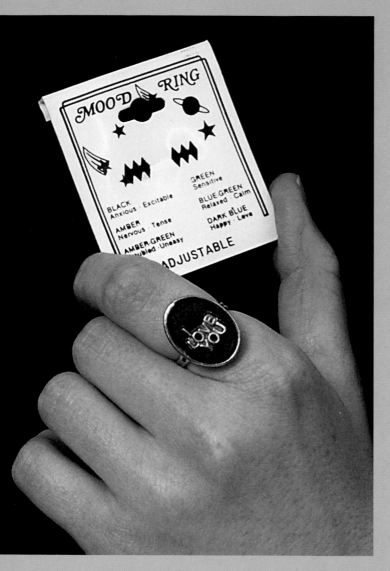

MOOD RINGS

Mood rings were rings that could tell what mood you were in. Quite amazing really, considering they were made of metal and coloured bits of glass. Black, for example, meant, 'I am angry'; green, 'I am happy'; blue, 'I want that Black Forest gateau off the dessert trolley', and so on. They had magical qualities, mood rings; it's amazing they've not come back into fashion. Then again, neither have alchemy and witch-burning.

Items C D E

tour de force honeysuckle

BATWING SLEEVES

A right-angled triangle is one where the square of the hypotenuse is equal to the sum of the squares of the opposite sides — or the shape of someone in batwings with one hand in the air. Big in the '80s, batwings were like a good dose of herpes: it took nearly a decade to get rid of them. More flying squirrel than your basic bat, batwings were like elongated flaps of skin linking the elbow, or sometimes the wrist, to the waist.

SIZES
8-16

ATLANTIS
FASHIONS

KNICKERBOCKERS

Loose-fitting breeches gathered at the knee or calf, knickerbockers were the leg fashion that meant you could ride a bike without resorting to cycle clips, and enjoyed a crushed-velvet comeback in 1982. Unfortunately for knickerbockers, chimney-sweep trouser legs reminded people more of workhouses and rickets than modern women, and they were thankfully retired to the great fashion chimney pot in the sky.

TIE DYE

This is when fashion was both affordable and a DIY project. Think The Grateful Dead meets Ben & Jerry's. Suddenly hippy teens the world over were holding hands and pouring huge churns of bleach and dye all over their clothes. Shirts, skirts, let's face it, clothing of every description, was put in a tub and streaked. Considered a bursting cornucopia of rainbow colour by some, tie dye made a generation look like a bag of shit.

BANDANAS

There was something contrived about bandanas. Folded in a triangle, wrapped round the forehead and then tied at the back, they gave guys that 'pirate meets Belarusian farmer's wife' look. Others folded into a simple headband but, if tied too tight, the eyebrows would be pulled so high that the wearer had a permanently startled expression.
Bandanas were favoured by Axl Rose and guys with George Michael stubble, gold hoop earrings and fake leopard-skin car-seat covers.

LEG WARMERS

The film *Fame* should be remembered for Leroy and for Irene Cara's theme tune, but it's the leg warmers that still stand out. Usually worn scrunched at the calf and pulled just under the heel, these socks without feet were all the rage in 1982; the fat-ankle look being just the thing. *Flashdance* delayed its death throes, but when leg warmers became the uniform of teenyboppers, no real dancer would be seen dead in them.

THE MIAMI VICE LOOK

In 1986, Don Johnson was the look: sweaters became shawls, sunglasses became headgear and everything was rolled up, particularly jacket sleeves and trousers — to expose sockless ankles and shins. Espadrilles, the sort of outdoor slippers an effete Kung-Fu master would wear to kickbox someone in the gut, were in. Made of canvas and costing less than a loaf of bread, their straw-like plaited soles had the consistency of bread too: one step in a puddle and they disintegrated.

CRIMPED HAIR

In the '80s, girls the world over fed their hair into the hairstyling equivalent of a sandwich toaster at a temperature high enough to smelt iron ore. Getting it right was an exact science, the permutations of which foxed many a teenage girl. Some stuck their fingers in electrical sockets to equal effect. Like poodles that had been zapped with cattle prods at the pet beauticians, many a crimp put joke-shop wigs to shame.

BOOTLACE TIES

George Michael has a sort of prairie-preacher thing going on here, or is it more Colonel Sanders from KFC? He looks like he would be better suited to handling a family bucket with fries and a tub of coleslaw than a glass of champagne. And what has he been doing with those curling tongs? These awful ties are now largely favoured by pensioners in places like Wigan and Telford line dancing to 'Achy Breaky Heart'.

FLUORESCENT LIPSTICK

In the '80s, heavy eyeshadow and orange lipstick was the look to have for people such as Sheena Easton and that half dummy/half woman thing from the film *Mannequin*. Orange lippy made women look like zombies in a straight-to-video gore movie. Or satsumas. In the '90s, Pamela Anderson opened her mouth wide for tit-pink lippy and for Tommy Lee, and fluorescent was back.

CULOTTES

Culottes: presumably the French for 'silly-looking'. Are these a skirt-cum-trousers or are they trousers-cum-skirt? Like a mix-up with the 'before' and 'after' pictures at Weight Watchers, this woman seems to be wearing the trousers she wore when she was 40 kilos heavier. Usually in flowery patterns, culottes flapped like curtains in the breeze. And, judging by the look of this pair, they appear to have enjoyed loyal service as a pair of curtains in a previous life.

FINGERLESS GLOVES

Defeating the whole point – keeping your fingers warm – fingerless gloves came in two distinct types in the mid-'80s: (1) knitted woollen, to give us that 'beggars sitting round a fire' look and a free finger to pick our noses with and (2) the see-through lacy netting ones as worn by Madonna in the 'Lucky Star' video. Pre-teen girls panic-bought fingerless fishnet gloves, exposed their belly buttons and vamped it up on street corners with crucifixes and boxing boots.

THE NEW ROMANTIC LOOK

Old Romantics, such as Keats and Shelley, wrote thoughtful poetry and lived lives dedicated to the ideals of Beauty and Truth. The New Romantics dressed up like transvestite pirates and ponced around on yachts. More concerned with their own reflection than inner reflection, the frilly shirts, bouffant hair, eye make-up and general 'been in the dressing-up box' look was just about forgivable in pop stars, but didn't go down quite so well in Dagenham.

SWEATBANDS

It wasn't just fuzzy perms that John McEnroe made fashionable in the '80s, but also terry cloth sweatbands. Teenage guys wore them while playing invisible guitars in front of their mirrors, thinking they were Mark Knopfler. Middle-agers had heart attacks in them step-kicking to the Jane Fonda workout. Then everyone realized they were just a towel that made your ears stick out, and they weren't cool anymore.

SILVER SHINY SUITS

Donny Osmond, hang your head in shame! Your sister Marie's range of porcelain dolls on the Shopping Channel is less overdressed than this fashion screamer. The shiny suit was a fashion cousin of the Miami Vice look. See how Donny's sleeves are rolled up to mid-forearm, his straight tie is loosely knotted, his hands are stuffed into pleated pants like he's playing pocket billiards, and the jacket is pushed behind. The suit radiates brightly, just like his teeth.

SHOULDER PADS

The icon of Thatcher–Reagan hubris, next to Chernobyl and cruise missiles, shoulder pads symbolized the '80s. Women everywhere looked like padded-up football players barging their way through shopping stores. We're talking *Dynasty* and *Dallas*, Alexis Carrington and Sue Ellen Ewing. If you turned round quickly in them you risked knocking a friend or work colleague unconscious in the process.

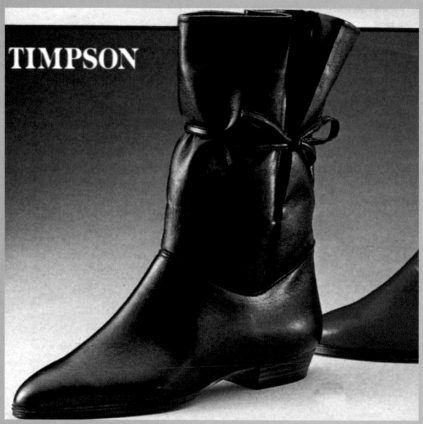

TIMPSON

PIXIE BOOTS

These wrinkly pull-on ankle boots somehow made women's feet look pig-like; they were too short and too wide fitting at the ankle so the leg seemed shorter than it was. Although called 'pixie' because they were supposed to look rascally and mischievous, they really looked like granny boots with zip-up sides and fur linings: practical and warm. All girls needed to complete the look were a pull-along shopping cart and a rain hat.

PUFFBALL SKIRTS

All the rage in the '80s and a close cousin of the ra-ra, the puffball was a skirt that was gathered in at the hem to give a balloon-like appearance. It looked like a woman in a ball gown had got her dress caught up in her underwear after a trip to the ladies' room. Generally, the ball shape isn't flattering, and puffballs made you look like an apple on legs. Still, these two old wallopers look like they know how to have a good time, eh?

RA-RA SKIRTS

Like a self-replicating puffball, the ra-ra was a series of puffy little layers. Girls tended to wear these circa 1982 with white ankle socks or leg warmers to look like cheerleaders, although they ended up looking more like can-can dancers or Havana prostitutes. If you spun round in one, you looked like a spinning top. Ra-ras came back with the Lambada dance craze in 1989, but they still looked like baby-girl tutus. Horrible.

HOME PERMS

In the '80s there were more DIY hair disasters than you could shake boxed home perm kits at, but they fell into three categories: (1) the 'curly', which doubled as a fright-wig you could go out trick or treating in; (2) the 'sheepskin shaggy', which made men look like Barbara Dickson and women like Brian May; and (3) the unclassifiable: the perm on the top, the gelled perm at the back, the fuzzball helmet and various combos thereof.

SKI-PANTS

These were trousers more suited to slaloming down the Matterhorn or doing an Eddie 'the Eagle' Edwards ski-jump, than the catwalk. Strange how a fashion item prefixed 'ski-' could look out of place where (a) there was usually no snow and (b) even if there was, there was not the slightest possibility of anyone actually skiing. Hooped under the foot with a stirrup, pulling ski-pants up was like playing a tug of war with your own body that you always ended up losing.

PUFFA JACKETS

If you were a skinny weakling, a puffa jacket made you look really hard and buff. It also made you look like a Soviet female shot-putter who had taken too many hormones and had developed testicles. Puffa jackets creaked and made us sweat profusely. They also tended to burst so that you shed feathers. Also, you'd only need a freak gust of wind and you and your puffa would be off on an Atlantic balloon-crossing challenge.

SNOODS

Originally an ornamental hairnet worn at the back of the head, by the '80s, snoods had evolved into tubes of knitted material that were worn as hoods. The overall affect was not dissimilar to a Cistercian monk with his habit hood up, or possibly the Grim Reaper. Snoods were usually too big and somehow looked floppy and silly as a consequence.

THE 'BODY'

The 'body' was like a leotard but had poppers or press studs at the crotch. The aim was to smooth out curves, but instead it made you look like a contestant in the one-woman luge going down the Cresta Run. In the '80s, every woman would squeeze herself into one of these Lycra body stockings, but if she knelt, bent over or coughed, the poppers would burst open. Many hours were subsequently spent in cubicles in the ladies' room, re-adjusting.

BUM BAGS

As attractive as a kangaroo's pouch, these originated in the '80s but were given a new lease of life in the '90s by clubbers and by holidaying pensioners. The bum bag (or fanny pack to Americans) had a handy zip-up compartment to store your chewing gum, money, drugs or false teeth. Shapeless and unflattering, they exaggerated the midriff like an add-on protruding gut. It's amazing that some saw fit to make a fashion feature out of them.

PUFF SLEEVES

High and loooo at the shoulder and tight from the elbow down to the wrist, every '80s Christmas-party frock had puff sleeves. They had all the aesthetic charm of water wings and made you look like one of those fat little fairies in Walt Disney's *Sleeping Beauty* or someone with deformed shoulder blades. Princess Diana was a big fan of puffed sleeves, but then again she loved puffs, full stop.

BERMUDA SHORTS

Loud and garish, traditional Bermuda shorts had prints of hanging palm trees set against a burning red sky, like a depiction of the Bikini Atoll atomic-bomb tests exploding all over your butt. More high street than beach bum, the market was flooded with rubbish versions so baggy that they fell down when we sneezed. With an inside netting, so that you didn't have to wear underpants, Bermudas chafed your inside leg something rotten.

BOMBER JACKETS

Originally intended for Second World War bombing raids, bomber jackets exploded onto the scene in the mid-'80s. Many were made not of leather but of cheaper polyvinyl chloride (PVC). When buttoned up, bomber jackets puffed out at the front to give you a bigger-looking gut; the tendency was to stuff your hands into the side pockets, further exaggerating this effect. Here, the jacket is worn with sensible slacks and a sweater for that ultimate smart-casual look.

JELLIES

Plastic transparent sandals; for some reason these highly affordable shoes took the '80s by storm. One downside was that they heated up and barbequed your feet. Another was that they also rubbed them so hard that the sides of your toes and the backs of your heels blistered and shaved off, so that your feet looked like they'd been put through a bacon slicer. The result wouldn't have looked out of place in a butcher's window.

HAWAIIAN SHIRTS

These could be classified under the general advisory heading, 'Fun clothes are not fun' or one entitled, 'Never mix comedy and fashion'. Traditionally the outfit of large American pensioners on vacation, Hawaiian shirts are both shapeless and garish, but still became big high-street fashion items in the early '80s. They looked cool in Waikiki, but the effect was lost standing inside a bus shelter in Birmingham. No real Hawaiian would actually be seen dead in one of these.

CYCLING SHORTS

Designed to decrease wind resist-ance during cycle races, in the '80s cycling shorts became fashionable in their own right. Cycling shorts showed more than the world needed to see and, as with all worst trends, those who really shouldn't have worn them were the ones who inflict-ed them on us. Everywhere, butts with the ballast of a ship were squeezed into neon skintight Lycra. The electric current generated from crossing your legs in cycling shorts would be sufficient to run a small heated towel rail.

SHELL SUITS

The worst fashion trend ever. We knew it at the time but zipped them up regardless. Like a crinkled stretch-fabric boiler suit in pastel colours such as spearmint green, dusky peach or powder blue, shell suits often came with clashing garish patterns down the sides of the legs, on the arms, or in random appliqué at the front and the back. Families in matching shell suits strolled through shopping malls together and walked straight into fashion disaster history.

APPLIQUÉ ON JUMPERS

Appliqué swept the globe in the '80s. No sweater, whether mohair, jersey or double knit, was spared the ravages of this ornamental needlework. Fabric, usually in pastel colours and in a material not dissimilar to your grandmother's old bedspread, was cut out and sewn to the surface of the aforementioned sweater, forming babyish pictures or patterns. And appliqué really did give a sense of the nursery: it looked like a baby had vomited all over you.

80

POLKA DOTS

There's something wrong with polka dots that you can't quite put your finger on. Perhaps polka dots remind us of a primeval time when early man was warned off eating spotty bugs or grubs. Or it could be the thought of the German Measles chasing across our faces as children. Or maybe it's that polka dots are just too loud: you see them before you see the clothes, and somehow that's not right.

STONEWASHED JEANS

As long as jeans weren't flared in 1980, anything went. Tight at the ankles, jeans came with paint and sparkly bits splattered on them, and were stonewashed, snow-washed or acid-washed. The big streaky bits of white gave the illusion that these jeans may have served a former owner loyally down a gold mine or cattle-rustling in the Wild West. Only they hadn't; we'd just had a bit of bleach tipped over them.

LEGGINGS

Leggings were like coloured tights that came halfway down your calf. These should strictly have been worn by women with slender thighs but, like all worst fashion trends, the sky blackened with ladies of a fuller figure fighting to get into them. Not unlike long johns and often worn only with a large baggy sweater or a coat, leggings gave the appearance that you'd left the house half dressed.

NON-MATCHING NEON SOCKS

In the mid-'80s, the 'non-matching neon sock' trend involved two pairs of socks, usually in terylene or terry cloth. The possibilities were endless: one yellow fluorescent sock with a luminous orange one, sizzling lime green and neon blue or maybe fluorescent pink. It really was amazing how this fashion trend didn't go on and on into perpetuity. And then we all came back to our senses and grey socks were appealing again.

BACKWARD BASEBALL CAPS

Originally enjoyed by skateboarders and teen posses, as with all the worst fashion trends, the 12-year-olds soon got hold of it. However, it was the 40-something men with ponytails and mid-life crises who provided the fatal blow to this particular gimmick. To out-manoeuvre the oldies, baseball caps were temporarily turned to one side or set on top of a bandana, but they never fully recovered from this fashion pummelling.

PARACHUTE PANTS

It's Hammertime! If there's one thing worse than a shell suit, it's a huge billowing shell suit. Remember MC Hammer's silver baggy trousers with the high waist? The kids who copied him thought they looked cool, but they just looked like tinfoiled oven-ready turkeys or like pensioners being treated for hypothermia. If they had carried around bicycle pumps, they could have had pantaloons permanently inflated to the size of a bouncy castle.

DUNGAREES

Dungarees are the fashion no-no that refuses to die. The unisex garb of '70s peace protests, dungarees made women look like painter-decorators. They came back in a street-gang form in 1982 when Dexy's Midnight Runners sang 'Eileen', but they never looked good. In the early '90s, we'd buckle up one side only or, with the help of a belt, leave the front and back flaps down, but there was no escaping it – they made the best of us look like inmates from *Prisoner Cell Block H*.

MULLETS

In '80s Britain, footballers Glen Hoddle and Chris Waddle popularized this hair-don't. It was known as the Eurotrash haircut in the United States — ironic, considering it only seems to have been sported by Michael Bolton and by rednecks throwing furniture at each other on Jerry Springer. Three hairstyles for the price of one: short and spiked on top, longer at the sides and finally, rat-tails dangling down past the neck. Horrible!

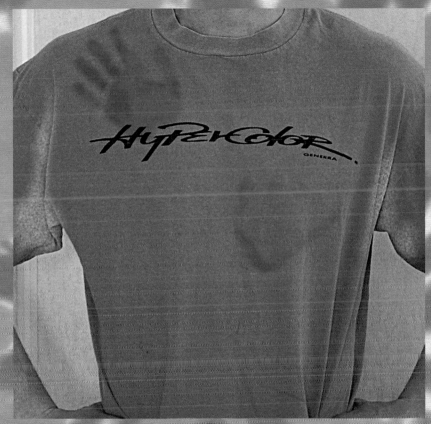

COLOUR-CHANGE T-SHIRTS

The mood ring of the fabric world, these T-shirts were made of material that changed colour according to the levels of heat on our bodies. The upshot was that your sweat patches were illuminated for the entire world to see. Huge swathes of tingling blue or red would glow under armpits and down backs. Like the plastic dresses of the '60s, this is another fashion trend led more by science than taste.

GOATEES

Goatees are so called because they make you look like a goat. Not the most flattering of animal-kingdom comparatives, it has to be said. While more hirsute guys held back from this trend, the pre-pubescent stormed in, cultivating their greasy whiskers so they looked more rat than man. Whether a moustache affair that descended, ramrod straight, to the chin or dangling down from the chin itself, goatees gave us all the look of Ming the Merciless.

GRUNGE

If you wanted to look good in 1991, you'd go to Seattle, help yourself to whatever you found in a dumpster and hang about looking suicidal. Grunge was dressing down, big style: ripped jeans, checked lumberjack shirts, big sweaters, heavy industrial shoes — and that was just the girls. The overall effect was that not only did we look like something from a dumpster, we smelt like it too.

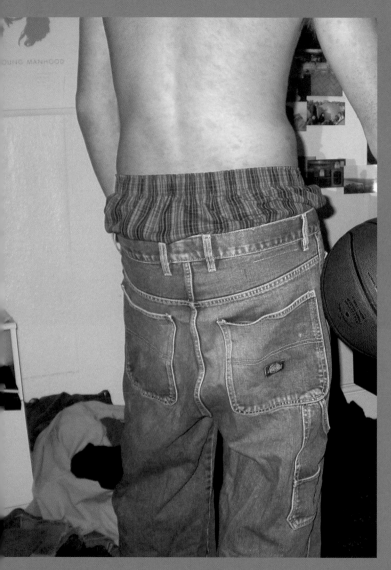

BAGGY JEANS

Flares may have gone out of fashion in the '70s, but in 1989, 21-inch Joe Bloggs jeans came back first with the Summer of Love and then again when Kris Kross wore all their clothes back to front in the video for 'Jump!' The key feature of low-slung jeans (also called 'shit-catchers') is showing off your underpants. The trouser choice of clowns and the morbidly obese, just because they're in now doesn't mean they're not bad — they're worse.

SARONGS FOR MEN

Men have worn dresses for centuries, and it usually led to their imprisonment. However, in 1998, football star David Beckham wore a sarong, and England's lads threw their trousers off with gay abandon, many looking more South Pacific drag act than Beckham. Sarongs demanded a good body but that didn't deter the lard-arses. Snag your sarong in the door and you'd be butt naked apart from your wooden beads.

FURTHER INFORMATION

www.advertisingarchives.co.uk
www.featheredback.com
www.uossnaps.co.uk/fashion
www.sixtiescity.com/Fashion/Fashion.htm
www.costumegallery.com/1960.htm
www.trackies.co.uk

BIOGRAPHY

Richard Jarman blames writing this book on an upbringing involving flares, parka coats and space-hoppers in the West Midlands in the '70s. He is a keen people-watcher and is author of *No Place Like Home* (New Holland).

PICTURE ACKNOWLEDGEMENTS

All photographs from The Advertising Archives except:
Richard Jarman p4(bottom), p5(top), p9; Alan Marshall p6, p15, p34, p37,
p42, p46, p48, p51, p59, p70, p72, p77, p80, p84, p89; Jenny Gimpel p17;
Popperfoto.com p18; Rex Features 2004 p21, p40, p54, p56, p60, p62, p65, p69,
p73, p74, p76, p83, p85, p87, p88, p90, p93; Donna Gallenberger p31;
Everynight Images / Alamy Images p33, Steve Skjold / Alamy Images p91;
Isabelle Baker p36, p41, p67; Gray Lappin p52; Top Foto / UPP 2004 p53,
John Paul Brooke / ScopeFeatures.com p71; David Parker p92

AUTHOR ACKNOWLEDGEMENTS

Special thanks to Abby and John Schoneboom and the rest of the New York City
posse at www.bonkworld.org for all their ideas. Many thanks also to Abby's
mum, Mrs Isabelle Baker, Jenny Gimpel, Donna Gallenberger, Kate Garoutte-
Smith, Gray Lappin and Robert Cluston for their hideous photos. Thanks also to
Ian Marchant, Jenny Mayor, David Parker, Phil Parvin, Carole Robinson and Karl
Sternberg.

This book is dedicated to my mum and to the fashion horror that was Pandora
catalogue clothing.

First published in 2005 by New Holland Publishers (UK) Ltd
London • Cape Town • Sydney • Auckland

10 9 8 7 6 5 4 3 2 1

www.newhollandpublishers.com

Garfield House, 86–88 Edgware Road, London W2 2EA, UK

80 McKenzie Street, Cape Town 8001, South Africa

14 Aquatic Drive, Frenchs Forest, NSW 2086, Australia

218 Lake Road, Northcote, Auckland, New Zealand

ISBN 1 84537 223 9

Publishing Manager: Jo Hemmings
Senior Editor: Kate Michell
Assistant Editor: Kate Parker
Cover Design and Design: Adam Morris
Production: Joan Woodroffe

Reproduction by Modern Age Repro House Ltd, Hong Kong
Printed and bound by Craft Print Pte Ltd, Singapore